Duration and
the Second Hand

Duration and
the Second Hand

Poems by Arthur Brown

David Robert Books

Published by David Robert Books
P.O. Box 541106
Cincinnati, OH 45254-1106

ISBN: 9781625490063
LCCN: 2012956064

Poetry Editor: Kevin Walzer
Business Editor: Lori Jareo

Visit us on the web at www.davidrobertbooks.com

For my good friends,
especially, this time, Arthur and Andy,
and, as always,
for Poem, Sadie, and Dmitri

Acknowledgments

"The Pantheist," "Houseflies." *The Carolina Quarterly* 61.3.

"Defenders of Wildlife: Florida Manatees," *American Literary Review* 21.1 (Spring 2010). Winner of the *American Literary Review* 2009 Poetry Contest.

"One-Act," AGNI 70 (2009).

"*Ora et Labora,*" *14 x 14*, March 2011.

"Philosopher," *American Arts Quarterly* 26.4 (Fall 2009).

"We are compelled to borrow from space the images by which we describe what the reflective consciousness feels about time and even about succession; it follows that pure duration must be something different."

— Henri Bergson, *Time and Free Will*

Table of Contents

I. Duration Sketches

Reception.. 15
One-Act... 16
Defenders of Wildlife: Florida Manatees.........17
Duration Sketches.. 19
The Art Spirit... 21
The Wake.. 24
Dissociation... 25
O... 26
From the Pub Balcony...................................... 27
Human Colors.. 28
From the Joan Marchand Bridge.....................29
Shadings... 31
The Crow.. 32

II. Second Hand Sonnets

The Second Hand.. 35
Wanderings... 36
First Avenue... 37
The Paperback.. 38
Professor Schmidt.. 39
Circle 2... 40
The Pantheist.. 41
Houseflies... 42
A Squeeze of the Hand..................................... 43
The Boards.. 44
The Glass.. 45
Abstract Expressionism.................................... 46
Low-Tide Man.. 47
Diagonal... 48

A Long Patience.. 49
Background and Figure.. 50
Ora et Labora... 51
Patrimony... 52
Merrily, Merrily, Merrily, Merrily...................... 53
Emergency Vehicle... 54
Alexander's Garage... 55
Old Man at the V.A... 56
Philosopher... 57
Violin.. 58
Steinway & Sons.. 59
In Memory, PDS, 1959-2012...............................60

III. The Beautiful White-Haired Lady

The Beautiful White-Haired Lady.................... 63

IV. Coda

We Three... 73

I. Duration Sketches

Reception

The whitewater now visible above
the spit of dunes—a constant overlap
of sound, not always audible, and wave
against the crows and busses starting up,
the children's cries, cicadas, chirping birds
that pass in little waves themselves instead
of glide, as if they're hobbled—thick as words
with sequence and the sense of something said.

The line of whitewater again, the roar
that strangely sounds mechanical without
the differentiation nearer shore
of overlap on overlap.

               The art's
in telling which is which—the musical,
the dissonant, the indivisible.

One-Act

You stand and watch, as from a balcony,
the waves break right to left and left to right
until they merge and form a line of white
diminishing—a scene repeatedly
played out; the shore's theatricality
that seems no less than ours, even the height
of drama, drama as the earthly rite
of motion, mass, and energy.
And then from left to right and right to left
along the sand, converging like the waves,
two runners, male and female, interposed
the human on the scene and, crossing, cleft
the backdrop painted there, upstaged the waves,
and drew a curtain that in parting closed.

Defenders of Wildlife: Florida Manatees

1.

Above them was the surface of the sea;
below it was direction and duration.
Rhythm, light, instantaneity
and in their world the sequence of creation.
Amorphous shapes of dark and lighter blue
cut by a swath of dark and lighter gray
that mirrored back the larger of the two
and turned to purely physical display
the subject of the photograph—
the journey of the mother and her calf
across the rock and sand horizon line
that cut the squared-off photograph in half
and deepened the symmetrical design
above the heading "June 2009."

2.

Above the heading "June 2009"
the unframed photograph was balanced by
a dark that seemed opposed to the design
and blurred the sand and rock horizon line
that marked the limit of the human eye
and of the lens and of the shutter speed,
and made the subject of the photograph,
the journey of the mother and her calf,
a thing in time, more difficult to read—
the medium of light and clarity
now foreground to a deep and opaque blue
below the changing surface of the sea,
that shaped, across its curving canopy,
the dark and light-gray passage of the two.

Duration Sketches

Seattle Asian Art Museum and Reservoir

1.

Grumbacher Prussian green, light green, chalk blue—
oil colors—olive, leaden green, zinc white
reflected from a sign, a silver pole,
the green from evergreens, the blue from sky;
zigzagging, interpenetrating light
through bracketed barbed wires, a chain-link grid:
"No Trespassing," the sign says—we just did
(above the words an icon of an eye
whose pupil is a painted water drop);
the radiating waves continuous,
contained within this concrete reservoir
that's sealed all round with calligraphic tar—
and held again in conscious fascination,
the permeable states of pure duration.

2.

Between the chain-link fence and concrete wall,
a male guard then a female make their rounds
in uniform—a work-shift change. And all
the while occur ten thousand sounds:
an airplane, then another, now a crow,
rolling down the grassy hill we go!
a dog, and earlier a fighting one
whose kindly master calmed it down below
Noguchi's 1969 *Black Sun*—
as constantly the fountain roars, the light
and form and movement interact.
Soundward, a helicopter still in sight—
out of the past, after the fact,
and tenuous against the blue and white.

The Art Spirit

"There are moments in our lives, there are
moments in a day, when we seem to see
beyond the usual. Such are the moments
of our greatest happiness. . . . If one could
but recall his vision by some sort of sign."
— Robert Henri

1.

The two-by-twelve had turned into a line,
its difference from the river going by
(although the water had a human air
so near the spillway and the DANGER sign)
and from the boulders and the dull gray sky
reflected in the river caught his eye
and made him momentarily aware
of something there beyond the usual
yet balanced in the horizontal plank—
transforming to invisibility
the visible, and making visible,
thanks to the distance that the river sank,
a depth impossible to see
except in signs, the bulk of which are blank.

2.

Against the emptiness of dull gray light,
the dark gray boulders lead to one
that holds a plank above the river's height.
A man downriver fishes with his son—
their poles extended, like the plank, in air,
but tapered, disappearing into lines
that slant toward something weighted there.
A cormorant extends its neck, defines
the water with a rapid slapping sound;
light turns to matter and the scene expands—
the bird now flying up and circling round
against the blending horizontal bands
of foreground, river, trees, and dull gray sky—
before a barge begins its going by.

3.

The father and the son stand arm-in-arm,
their fishing and the passing of the barge
allied like levee rocks against the harm
to come—of disaffection, life at large;
the scene already stuff of memory,
existing more in observation than
in matter, more in what they cannot see
behind them or ahead than what they can:
the wake of roiled white-water diminished
hump by hump though never ending, first
becoming last, until it's only finished
going by—and father-son immersed
in other things than fishing at that spot;
one looking back to see what they forgot.

The Wake

Out of the landscape, moving in it now,
the barge appears to have no end—
a medium through which time's passage slows
and can be counted: 3 abreast, 5 deep,
a quarter-mile long from stern to bow,
the contradictory towboat pushing, manned
apparently (behind the long windows)
but in itself a loud, imposing presence
rivaling the river's endlessness,
although the trail of whitewater won't keep
its variation from the river—less
a marker than a disappearance
into light on an unsteady, changing base
and shadows likewise taking place.

Dissociation

May 2008

Driftwood lies promiscuous as bones—
the dead in one another's arms, the moans
of men and women halfway round the world.
Between his grandparents a child curled
and waited for the excavator's hand.
The driftwood lifts and falls against the sand.
Appalling post-disaster metaphor,
yet real corpses feel no more than this
mere human-looking wood—nor hold, nor kiss.
Nor can a living man be moved much more
by what he's heard all week on NPR
of deaths in Sichuan and Myanmar.
The river drifts from left to right, the swallows
dally, bank, and turn—the river follows.

O

"Now thou Art an O Without a Figure."
—Shakespeare, *King Lear*

Hexagonal brick, a red dividing line;
beyond, a strip of clover blossoming—
and then, below the bank's unseen decline,
the sheen of river, barely lightening
where gaps between the far bank's trees let shafts
of sky across the horizontal reach.
The distant speedboat and its rubber raft
make double-Vs—sun-spangled wakes that breach
the blankness left and right—until an arc
of spray precedes a flying rubber O
whose rider had to disembark
by some mistake, apparently, although
no rider's seen; the speedboat circles round—
a focal point against unmanned background.

From the Pub Balcony

We watch the barge to watch the barge begin
and slowly end—trees backing off the plank
against the far Ohio River bank,
whose steeples, stacks, and silos shadow in
the towboat bridge, so that the long, flat barge
that has to stiffly make the horseshoe turn
appears (a headless length, tailed by the churn
of yellow-brown Ohio wake) too large;
and yet it slowly does, and reappears
out of the stand of willows, barely fitting
whole between it and the ever-sitting
steamboat stern with which it now collides,
diminishing—as we all drink our beers—
before it finally absolutely hides.

Human Colors

Memorial Day Weekend

Three abreast, the bow irregular—
one barge-head curved and femininely waked
by yellow-brownish curls of whitewater,
the buoy on its far side lightly rocked;
the cargo-covers ribbed, the passage slow—
the barges rust-streaked, red, green, orange, gray,
five-deep, inexorably moving—

                    tow-
boat pushing aft: white-diamond flagged and gaily
trimmed in human colors, like
the teal and lilac splattering the dike,
the toddler-pink and mustard-yellow bike,
that pass from right to left and left to right
more quickly than the barge—

                        that's still in sight,
upriver, in the distance, black and white.

From the Joan Marchand Bridge

1.

One kid sits backward on the handle bar
and pedaling backward tows a bigger kid
who suicidally steers a plastic car
across the steel truss bridge behind your head
and sings a line on which he's stuck
that sounds like, "Shorty wants to fuck, fuck, fuck."
You draw the Xs of the bolted grid,
the trusses of the bridge heartbreaking red,
the horizontal lines of bank and rail,
the tow—its barges red, black humps of coal—
the towboat and the churning trail
of backwater. You want to get it whole:
the ragged skyline of Kentucky trees
and what the kid on his back behind you sees.

2.

You want to get it whole—the passing tow
(this one from right to left and moving fast),
two empty yellow barges moored below
the bridge, the wider span of sunlight cast
on iron, stone, and bolted bright-red truss;
three women and a man, his cigarette,
the train, the grain conveyor silhouette,
the changing character and calculus
of light and sound and interval—
the water refluent and yellow-lit,
sky-brown and shadow-brown; and under it
a movement endlessly replaceable
that's never whole and never otherwise—
you watch it wrinkle, swirl, and spiralize.

Shadings

"Is it a boat? Is it a cask?"
—Virginia Woolf, *To the Lighthouse*

The higher consciousness—the lower, too—
is measureless, the permeable states
of pure duration, as the sea's not blue
but shadings from the lightest blue to slate,
and time's without extension, quality
not quantity—a matter of the mind
that knows the wave's not where it used to be
but left something, a speck of red, behind.
And there's the mischief—to confuse the two:
time's heterogeneity with space;
succession, rhythm, all things that accrue,
all melody, with stopping points—replace
the fascination of the visual
with soundings, syllable by syllable.

The Crow

"The conclusion of this discussion is that so
far as sense-awareness is concerned there is
a passage of mind which is distinguishable
from the passage of nature though closely
allied with it."

— A. N. Whitehead

"It is an exhibition of the process
of nature that each duration happens and"—
there sped a clapping shadow, as if hands
(deformed and oddly angled down) had passed
the square-glass paneled double-doors and blocked
the light in such a way that made it flash
peripherally—accompanied by sound
just after or before, I can't recall,
for I was reading at the time. And now
in time I've doubled back and held in thought
that brief event, as if I'd trained the crow
to capture my attention, squawk and fly
(or, flying, squawk) and, clapping, shadow in
this special reciprocity of being.

II. Second Hand Sonnets

The Second Hand

The gambler's gamble is the flush or straight,
where one card renders each that came before
the precedent of something more—and more
than all its parts. A whole—or nothing.

Another drink! Submerge my consciousness
in stimulant, sensation, things discrete
that can't, except mechanically, repeat.
The second hand! Without experience.

A pair? Two pair? Is that the hand I'm dealt?
High card? Three of a kind? The cards are laid
face down; I turn them spade, by spade, by spade
and feel a shock each time almost electric.

Tick, tick-tick, tick-tock, and then a stroke
of luck—the charm of formlessness—a club.

Wanderings

The day'd been windy, cold, the sun descending
brightly now on hard-packed sand and water.
One more Christmas past—the year was ending;
behind him on the beach, his wife and daughter.

Ahead a woman in her youth approached
in woolen, tapered overcoat—alone.
His interest roused immediately, he coached
himself so that his manner might atone
for lapses past, and present, too, in mind.

He looked in her direction, smiled.

                                    "Hi,"
she said.

          The sun had made him almost blind.
"Hi. How are you?"

                    "Good," she said.

                                While he
remembered avenues like desert shores,
and naked light bulbs, dead-end corridors.

First Avenue

The manikin across the street behind
the glass of her window and mine
is wearing something blowing in a wind;
my candle flickers, rims my glass of wine.

The window spells out backwards *Le Pichet*.
A V-necked woman with her boring friend
laughs happily, drinks her wine; she doesn't mind
he's boring or I'm watching—cants her pitcher.

Today it rained. I shivered on the lake.
I drink espresso with a lemon rind,
a Scotch—the waitress takes my demitasse.
The V-necked woman poses for my sake.

Outside, the vagrants looking through the glass
for their own part could use a little class.

The Paperback

The book was *The Voyeur* by Robbe-Grillet—
the first or last book on the shelf behind
a metal bookend. In the light of day,
half-nude, back toward the louvered window blind,
thumbs in her skirt-band, one knee on the bed,
a girl who seemed alone and yet aware
someone was watching.

                  Someone was, who'd read
the book whose cover made him put it there
behind the bookend's dark green arch that framed
her tartan skirt, bare arms, and yellow hair.

When he took down the book to free the girl,
an imprint of the bookend arch remained:
overexposed, the slender paperback
had fixed the reader in its own dark look.

Professor Schmidt

And how could he, Professor Schmidt, admit
that reading, too, had turned into a vice
that turned on him—a thing he couldn't quit,
like cigarettes or something not as nice.
In afternoons he lingered in the shops
imagining the things he'd never buy,
where pretty girls took off their pretty tops
through curtains in the corner of his eye.
There must be places for such men as he,
out of the way—a weedy park, or jail,
or by-the-month a bungalow by the sea;
what he wanted was to go somewhere and fail.
Or should he close the book with suicide?
A thing almost impossible to hide.

Circle 2

"That day we read no further"
— Dante

The sense of love is possibility—
pursuit of someone not yet turned around.
You change directions; nobody can see
the part of you gone underground
and damned, past hope, divided from
the curb, the Lutheran church across the street
that sees before it only what's to come,
though still you keep your distance and your feet;
as she her pace, her ponytail aswirl,
clip-clopping past the parking lot,
a nice, you're sure, you're sure a pretty girl
you think a stranger, till you see she's not—
when safely in her car she turns her head
and smiles benignly at the living dead.

The Pantheist

"But while this sleep, this dream is on ye,
move your foot or hand an inch; slip your
hold at all; and your identity comes back in
horror."
      —Melville, *Moby Dick*

He climbed the hill intent on suicide
as young men sometimes are—not half believing,
having much to live for, nothing much to hide,
just this romance in the abstract with grieving.
Below him lay the reddening wilderness—
behind, the winding road, the dam and lake,
whose sounds, just like the trail, grew less and less.
On a white-washed rock he paused for pausing's sake.

And then he heard, as if it brushed his neck,
the wind-ripped pinions of a vulture's wings—
watched it circle round, death's-head back-bended,
inquiring of the canyon for some wreck
it might explore. And he, his wanderings
dead-ended, for the time being, descended.

Houseflies

You use the child's room upstairs—it's bright.
The house is heated by a stove; at night
it's cold. Your days are numbered like the flies'.
You have some work to finish; otherwise,
you've had about enough of solitude.
And when the buzzing frantically intrudes
on mountain ranges, woods, and unmowed grass,
you make a constellation on the glass
in negative—black stars backlit by day,
one twinkling till you take the thing away—
and drive to town to watch the game and drink
with strangers. Strangely coming back to think
there's someone in the house, a homely presence—
the breadth of death above the night's indifference.

A Squeeze of the Hand

Hidden, or projected, grief sometimes appears
in dreams, where those who seem in life to be
mere caricatures, our former friends or peers,
lose all their ghastly personality
and weep, their eyes on ours unashamed,
so that we see, as if it were our own,
the humanness behind the blackly framed
thick glasses underneath the sloping bone
of forehead; recognize the two-way lie
of their indifference and our perception.
And then the workplace grin and waking eye
become an almost rational deception,
so odd it is to squeeze the fellow's hand
and feel the slackness that leaves us all unmanned.

The Boards

"Water, water, every where,
And all the boards did shrink . . ."
—Coleridge, *The Rime of the Ancient Mariner*

High school teachers kissing paper boys
and shouting, "Fire!"—then regaining poise
while luck's expended in a poker game;
the colored lights will never be the same.

Two suitcases too full, a mended stocking,
elms cut down, a tape recorder mocking;
life's "a casting off," a father's flute,
and everybody finally in a suit.

Rothschild's fiddle, Cash's graphophone—
life's measured by the coffins that we own.
A blinded Oedipus, a weeping Lear—
an actor practicing the look of fear.

And for the mariner, the albatross.
Man's only profit is the song of loss.

The Glass

I'd been in charge that day of venues—and
for months it stood there on my desk: the glass
that Arthur Miller drank from that my hand
had held with his. It made me feel an ass—
unlike the Covent Garden mug, the coaster
stolen from a Suffolk pub, the rocks
and shards and scallop shells, the Graham Greene poster,
though this last bears something too that mocks
the hero worshipper, the amateur,
and holds a mirror up to what I'm not.
Some keepsakes keep the secrets of our wishes;
others only whisper what they were
before the spirit-part began to rot.
Tonight I washed it with the other dirty dishes.

Abstract Expressionism

He finished it, then walked around it, stopped,
and though an hour ago it hadn't seemed
an error, took his hammer up and lopped
a chunk the size of Texas off—redeemed
the whole endeavor. Then sat down and took
his eyes away, as if renouncing drink,
tobacco, sex with. . . . No. He had to look.
The last thing he should do, he knew, was think—
but from this angle, too, something was wrong
he couldn't put in words that made him see
what had been staring at him all along:
a figure, naked, sitting silently
inside the contours of the thing. And then—
he finished it again, again, again!

Low-Tide Man

I passed a whelk, pool-buried in the sand,
then turned and doubled-back to dig it out,
the animal a fat-lipped water spout
I thought I'd kindly lend a human hand
to toss it—lifesaver-like—deeper in
the lowest tide I'd seen that holiday.
It might have lived without me, who could say?
I passed a starfish, pipers, gulls—and then
some crude graffiti stick-drawn in the sand
to penisize the vast and vacant beach
and claim a corresponding human reach.
I could have trampled it but let it stand,
so monumentally it lay—
upon the beach a quarter of a day.

Diagonal

"For all have doubts, many deny; but doubts
or denials, few along with them have
intuitions."
                                        —Melville, *Moby Dick*

Leaning back in your chair, your arms out wide—
a gesture made at first without intent—
you joked last night that you'd been crucified.
Your wife, across from you, knew what you meant.

And now, still on this long slow walk alone
through woods not far removed from humankind,
you stop—leaf-fall, birdsong, even the drone
of some machine seem of one peaceful mind—
and almost think you know what people mean
by—

        And then the guy wire of the radio tower,
transfixed against the blue above the green,
takes all the evidence of higher power,
all you might have taken for a sign,
into its own steel-straight diagonal line.

A Long Patience

*"Le talent est une longue patience. . . . Il y
a, dans tout, de l'inexploré."*
— Maupassant

In its black reflective bowl, diurnal time—
the grass, the image of the tulip tree—
and in the round ash-bearing dog-bit tray
a buried black Lab memory.
Within the dome, the charcoal record of
the fish and flesh and fowl—the life
transmissible, as in a narrative,
through death—long since consumed and carried off.
Below them, on the two-wheeled tripod rack,
the handle, shield, and chimney at a slant:
the moon in phases, a horizon line,
a spray-paint silver sea, rust swirls on black.
And in the sunlit web from leaf to grill,
the storyteller's art, the painter's skill.

Background and Figure

After he won the Sixth, he walked to backs
of owners, cousins, friends—whoever they were—
on the oval grass enclosure. Left, the track's
brown dirt; the columned paddock, right. The blur
of Triple Crowns he'd come from behind to win
or lose surrounding him in some cool mix
of history, artifice, and silks. His grin
as Cajun as on TV. Just for kicks
about to ride a camel between races.
And the camels—numbered, bridled, being led
around him and around, with cartoon faces,
humps, and iron saddles—disappeared.
We didn't notice till Borel had gone
and the camels and the racetrack came back on.

Ora et Labora

I passed him gardening in his yard by light
from an electric cord. Ahead a man
came from the dark of what seemed more than night—
of alcohol: a darkness that began
some time ago, by the dark look of him,
the slant and stagger of his form, a face
that seemed an amputated limb,
and the dripping torture of his slow bent pace.
And yet the gardener made no sign of hearing,
kneeling in his pool of light, the nearing
stranger; did not look up from his labor—
recognizing that slow shuffling sound
and not the fear in which I'd turned around
and made a murderous drunkard of his neighbor.

Patrimony

My good friend tried to get it—what he felt
on seeing, side by side, my son and me;
not peeking at the cards the kid was dealt
but stepping back, soul-patched and painterly.
He looked around for help. None came.
He said my son had turned into my equal.
We sidestepped, swaggered, chuckled—pretty lame;
but near enough, he meant, to know the sequel.
So we left it there, at my niece's wedding.
Till he wrote back in a letter with the heading
"Martha's Vineyard," and my neighbor and his son
walked by: dog on the leash, son on the phone
(a tall young man who'd moved out years ago),
and my neighbor dragging—past the front window.

Merrily, Merrily, Merrily, Merrily

We meet the other novices, give three
a ride—I can't think of their names: the one
from Costa Rica, one from Austin (he
is talking)—up in front I'm with my son;
we're following the coxswain's Subaru,
her bumper stickers what you might expect,
Rainier in clouds now, south toward Portland to
the lake; at close to five the water flecked
with gold—then darkly rippling and wet
as shivering from the coach's launch I watch
alongside starboard then alongside port
and roaring up behind until I get
the terms "release" and "feathering" and "catch"
under a double rainbow youth and sport.

Emergency Vehicle

The ambulance that crossed Green River Road
had waited for the light to change, unlit
and unannounced, a van without a load—
and yet some knowledge seemed to follow it.
No one pulled over, no one had to stop
along his way. But I was not alone,
I'll bet, in letting my attention drop
into an unmarked meditative zone—
beneath the frequencies of radios
and booming, multi-colored, optical
distractions heightening our to-and-fros
through town—and seeing, in that vehicle,
the seated figure of emergency
rotund and smug with possibility.

Alexander's Garage

Diminished on the gurney, as you'd lie
at home in bed, aslant and toward one side—
but in a bag, sealed up, wheeled backward by
a bald man through a door. A private ride
before the next-to-last and last (unless
you count the lowering) to burial.
Not many tasks remaining: this, to dress
the corpse, and that, to say the usual.

I didn't know the man or woman dead
but had this glimpse of death—contemporary.
No soul idling in the garage; instead,
the body bagged and almost good to bury—
wheeled backward by a bald man through a door.
No waiting for the ferry at the shore.

Old Man at the V.A.

"If only he'd not been there!"
— Ovid

His arteries had hardened—circulation
poor, they had to amputate his leg.
And when they had, the comfort of relation
left him. "Muh, muh, muh, muh, muh," he begged
of wife and son and daughter—anyone
who could restore his wholeness or reduce
the pain. No one could touch him, though his son
reached down and stroked his forehead, brushed the loose
white hair. No one could answer to those eyes,
ice blue, that stared and stared but couldn't say—
the eyes of that young hunter in disguise
who'd seen too much before he'd turned away;
still there—though changed in life and limb—
until his dogs caught sight of him.

Philosopher

All that talk of dying gone from him;
the brief eternal readiness was all
he wanted—slipping from the interim
of love. Adrift, or almost, he'd recall
that doctrine of Aurelius—that men,
regardless of their time on earth, were last
year's leaves: you had your generation, then
another its, and so the drama passed.
What of it—if the calm directing mind
could say, "I am in keeping of my own,
I recognize in other men my kind,
in all of nature Wholeness." Yet his tone
was off. The leave-taking of wife and daughters
waked him from his meditative waters.

Violin

"My next life I'll apprentice in a shop,"
he thought, on seeing something nicely made
behind the glass in the museum amid
the paintings and the furniture. To shape
something by hand—it seemed a worthy aim
till now too plain for his abstracted mind.
Once for all to be a maker, manned
by skill; not say, "I think, therefore I am"
but *do*, and in so doing—using tools
to measure, cut, and fasten ("theme"
gone by the board with "truth" and "meaning")—*be*,
as artful as the artifact that tells
the facts of life by being one of them,
a player needing neither bow nor bow.

Steinway & Sons

Three women: violinist, pianist,
and page-turner—this last anonymous,
reading for the pianist and us;
poised, as they were, with a practiced hand and wrist,
but silent, never idle, all in black,
as they were; not reflected in the tile
that made a pool out of the center aisle—
bodiless, unsequined, further back;
the first on stage, houselights to half, to place
the sheet music and play a note with a look
to the wings. Her bench aslant, she stayed on book
with something like a sacrificial grace—
all instrument, without the lettering
Steinway & Sons, all perfect rendering.

In Memory, PDS, 1959-2012

He died in the prime of life, a journalist,
and all his friends were at the funeral:
talented people, people who could talk—
who'd worked with him for years and gotten pissed
with him at the Vat and Fiddle and paid the bill
and kidded with his kids on a Sunday walk.
And really got to know him and his wife
the day they said good-bye to him for life—
and then they lost it, couldn't talk at all;
the training they'd got at the BBC
went out the window; every elegy
that started ended in a dying fall.
We listened to his favorite sound—the call
of seagulls. Then we listened to the sea.

III. The Beautiful White-Haired Lady

The Beautiful White-Haired Lady

1.

"My life's so weird," she said. "It's just so weird."
For still, at 82, green-eyed, white-haired,
she'd make a young man turn his head
and say, "You know, you're a very beautiful woman."
Though nothing, nothing turned out as she'd hoped.
"It's such a stupid life." She was alone.
She'd had a love affair with someone famous—
famous terribly and tragically—
and hadn't anything to show for it;
for anything—but books, her love of authors:
Conrad, Henry James; her manuscripts,
sent out, returned unread, or read by those
who loved her work and knew (and wished her well)
not in a million years could her book sell.

2.

"I must look like I'm smiling—people smile
at me when I walk down the street."
They hadn't seen her vomit at the circus
when her aunt and uncle took their princess to
the House of Freaks—the childless millionaires,
Aunt Sadie and Uncle Sydney of New York;
who left her in the will she'd waited for
the jewelry that her Uncle Albert took,
the share she lost when she divorced, and not
the bonus they'd provided Mark's first son,
their "godson." Why was she less clever than
her brother, less conniving—less successful?
Although the greatest thing he did was move
to Mulholland so she could find true love.

3.

He walked into the den, then took her for
a motorcycle ride: this wallflower,
this smiling, green-eyed sis, this divorcée.
This mother, incidentally, of three.
"We slid down on our *fannies*," she would say—
his word, not hers; the three of us could tell.
She told us everything. "You coming up?"
he'd ask at two a.m. Most times she would,
for acrobatics, poetry recitals,
mood swings, sleep—the whirligig of love.
And then Coldwater Canyon's winding down
in her yellow Mustang to West Hollywood,
a bath, her children, IBM again—
and the long comparison to other men.

4.

And now she was alone, for actors, too,
can die—and do. Twice-over not a widow,
since divorcées have given up that right
and would-be wives or mistresses don't have it.
In Santa Fe. What's Santa Fe to her?
Even the in-laws of her middle son—
her two best friends—were gone or halfway gone:
Rina now in Santa Clara Pueblo
and Ralph, though both were 10 years younger, dead
of prostate cancer that they might have cured—
a man whom she could really drink and talk with;
no one had ever made her feel so smart.
Although he'd say, "Come off it, Harriette!"
and unlike others got away with it.

5.

The novel ends in suicide. You make
your life, the famous actress knew, a story
or a bore. The novel's other character,
an actor, too, survives—or dies before;
you'd have to ask the author or someone
who read the manuscript more recently
than I, the younger son—the published one.
Of the older she is also proud—the doctor.
And her daughter, too—who in her childhood had
imaginary horses, Tired and Weak,
and two friends, one named Frère, one named Jacques.
A painter for a time—who, like her mother,
knows that there are things one can't transcend.
And wonders, too, how does the *memoir* end?

6.

After the circus and Aunt Sadie's will,
the 12-year marriage, single parenthood,
the 2 a.m. telepathy (sometimes
without a speaker on the other end—
a solitary ring she knew was him),
what *was* there? Her father's Alzheimer's,
her mother's brain tumor, the split from Mark,
the moves from West L.A. to West L.A.
to West L.A to San Francisco then
(after the money came) to Marblehead—
the house, the drop-seat jumpsuit misadventure—
Santa Fe, then back to Hollywood
to work for Marlon as his more-than-friend,
then Santa Fe again? Was *that* the end?

7.

It wasn't over yet. She thought she'd like
to try New York once more—another long shot.
But this time, not the Bronx or Hunter College.
If only she'd gone into publishing
back when her mother said it was the men
who were the breadwinners and sent her son
upstate to Syracuse to meet his wife
(the only thing that *she* had over her
was seeing *Streetcar* at the Barrymore)
and study architecture. Still, if he'd
not moved to Mullholland ("The lights you see!
The lights of all L.A.!" her mother gushed)
then Marlon wouldn't have walked into the den.
And now, besides, she loved her grandchildren.

8.

So there she was—this white-haired lady whom
young men would see as someone otherworldly.
"It's just so weird." She meant the contradiction.
For what they saw, she knew, was like a truth
that all the world conspired against. She, too,
turned everything she touched to shit—a phrase
she used to use. "Someday he'll come along"—
that was another and our favorite one.
But no, he never did. And how to tell
someone that *that* was how it was in all
the books she loved—that *that* and not the wish
was truth—and that the beast had sprung? And yet
she knows. She's not a witch. She's just alone.
But not, my mother, *all* alone.

IV. Coda

We Three

"How, now, my hearts! Did you never see
the picture of 'we three'?"
                    —Shakespeare, *Twelfth Night*

The clown that rode through Central Park
made three balls arc
in opposite directions, each
beneath the one that came before,
while pedaling a bicycle—
and managed somehow, too, to reach
the lever on the handlebar
that trilled the silver bell.
He seemed in passing there to take
(for his own or for heaven's sake)
the measure of all human evanescence;
nodded, too, to say to me,
in mildly mocking mummery,
"The universe acknowledges your presence."

Arthur Brown's first book of poems, *The Mackerel at St. Ives*, was published by David Robert Books in 2008. He has published poems in *AGNI, American Arts Quarterly, American Literary Review, The Carolina Quarterly, Dogwood, Michigan Quarterly Review, The Malahat Review, The Raintown Review, Poetry, Southwest Review*, and other journals, and his poems have won the Morton Marr Poetry Prize, the Nebraska Shakespeare Festival Anne Dittrick Sonnet-Writing Contest, and the *American Literary Review* Poetry Prize. His one-act play "Augustina" was selected by Horton Foote as the winner of the *Arts & Letters* Drama Prize. He has published literary essays on Poe, Henry James, Faulkner, and Shakespeare. He is a professor of English at the University of Evansville.

CPSIA information can be obtained at www.ICGtesting.com
Printed in the USA
LVOW130108230113

316850LV00001B/4/P